T0165072

THE UNOFFICIAL HARRY POTTER-INSPIRED BOOK OF COCKTAILS

Fantastic Drinks and How to Make Them

RHIANNON LEE & GEORGIA HINGSTON

PHOTOGRAPHY BY ALINE SHAW

Skyhorse Publishing

Copyright © 2021 by Rhiannon Lee and Georgia Hingston
Photography copyright © 2021 by Aline Shaw

All rights reserved. No part of this book may be reproduced in any manner without the express written consent of the publisher, except in the case of brief excerpts in critical reviews or articles. All inquiries should be addressed to Skyhorse Publishing, 307 West 36th Street, 11th Floor, New York, NY 10018.

Skyhorse Publishing books may be purchased in bulk at special discounts for sales promotion, corporate gifts, fund-raising, or educational purposes. Special editions can also be created to specifications. For details, contact the Special Sales Department, Skyhorse Publishing, 307 West 36th Street, 11th Floor, New York, NY 10018 or info@skyhorsepublishing.com.

Skyhorse® and Skyhorse Publishing® are registered trademarks of Skyhorse Publishing, Inc.®, a Delaware corporation.

Visit our website at www.skyhorsepublishing.com.

10 9 8 7 6

Library of Congress Cataloging-in-Publication Data is available on file.

Cover design by Daniel Brount
Cover photo by Aline Shaw

Print ISBN: 978-1-5107-6524-5
Ebook ISBN: 978-1-5107-6525-2

Printed in China

This book is dedicated to anyone who still hasn't given up hope that their Hogwarts acceptance letter may be coming by owl—and plans on getting smashed while they wait!

Those wishing to indulge in the libations herein must be of legal drinking age.

Underage witches and wizards found in the possession of this book will be brought in front of a disciplinary hearing. The accused will undergo thorough interrogation. Those found guilty of underage drinking could face up to five years in prison, along with confiscation and destruction of wands and cocktail shakers.

Excessive drinking may lead to side effects similar to those who have been hexed. Therefore, please drink responsibly and in moderation, so to prevent emergency trips to hospital.

It is also imperative that drinkers do not operate any enchanted vehicles or brooms while under the influence of alcohol.

Always . . . stay safe.

Contents

Part I

Introduction

This is the essential guide for conjuring up the perfect cocktail, so whether you're charming guests at a Halloween party, or you simply live every day as if you're in the wizarding world, this is the perfect recipe book for you.

All the bewitching recipes in this book are based on classics but have been given a magical makeover. With the use of novel ingredients, fabulous flare, and a bit of science magic, you'll soon be transforming the mundane into masterpieces of mixology. Unique ingredients such as activated charcoal, popping candy, and dry ice make these cocktails anything but ordinary.

With potions and elixirs for all levels, you can easily summon something simple and tasty or put your skills to the test and conjure up a cocktail that is truly magical. Helpful bartending tips throughout give you the tools to conquer the dark arts of mixology.

Pull up a bar stool at the Leaky Cauldron and enjoy a cocktail or two because every witch, wizard, squib, or muggle deserves that magical feeling of finding their perfect cocktail.

Sincerely yours,
Rhiannon and Georgia

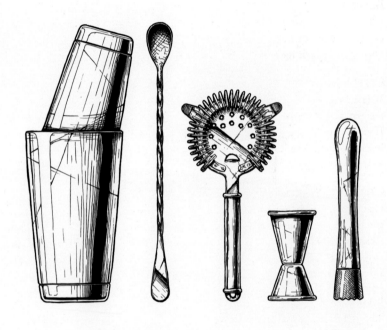

Basic Equipment

Bar Spoon
The classic bar spoon has a long, twisted handle, a flat end, and a tear-drop-shaped spoon used for measuring out and stirring spirits.

Blender
An electric blender is required for some recipes involving fruit and ice cubes. It doesn't need to be an expensive or powerful blender, just good enough to crush ice.

Citrus Squeezer
When making delicious cocktails using fresh citrus, juice is crucial. A citrus squeezer can really save time and ensure that you get every last drop. If you don't have a squeezer, simply use your hands. Tip: To get the most juice, roll the fruit in the palm of your hands, slice it in half, and microwave for five seconds. Then, simply use a fork to squeeze the juice out.

Cocktail Shaker
Coming in all different shapes and sizes, the standard shaker is stainless steel with three parts: a base known as a "can," a built-in strainer, and a cap (which can be used as a jigger). It's brilliantly straightforward and easy to keep clean. If you can't get your hands on a cocktail shaker, consider using a large glass jar with a lid and waterproof seal.

Jigger
The jigger is the standard measuring tool for spirits and liqueurs, and a toolbox essential for any avid cocktail maker. If you don't have a jigger, a single shot glass or even an eggcup can be a stand-in. In this book, one shot is measured as I oz. (30 milliliters).

Muddler
To extract maximum flavor from certain fresh garnishes such as mint or fruit, use a muddler to crush the ingredients. If short a muddler, a fork and some gentle poking is a good substitute.

(Continued on next page)

STRAINER

Most cocktail shakers are sold with a built-in strainer. However, if yours doesn't have one, any fine mesh strainer works just as well. Tip: when a cocktail calls for straining, ensure that you've used ice cubes, as crushed ice tends to clog the strainer in standard shakers.

How To

To make the perfect cocktail, you don't need to be a fully trained wizard juggling lemons and flipping bottles. The reality is much simpler and with these tricks anyone can create cocktail magic!

Layer
Some drinks call for a careful layering of ingredients to create an ombré effect. Always start with the heaviest liquid (with the most sugar content). To add a second layer, place a spoon upside down inside the glass, but not touching the first layer of alcohol. Very slowly pour the second liquid over the back of the spoon to form a distinct second layer. Repeat for subsequent layers.

Rim
To add an extra flourish to a drink, the rim of a cocktail glass is often decorated. To achieve this, spread a few tablespoons of the desired ingredient onto a small plate. Moisten the outer rim of the glass with water, a citrus-wedge, or syrup. Then, roll the outer rim of the glass on the plate until lightly coated. Hold the glass upside down and tap to release any excess.

Shake
When a cocktail contains eggs, fruit juice, or cream, it is necessary to shake all the ingredients. It not only mixes the ingredients, but also chills them simultaneously. When shaking a cocktail, there is no agreement on the perfect time, but ten seconds of brisk shaking is recommended.

Stir
Using a bar spoon (or wand!), stir the drink and ice gently together to chill the concoction. When condensation forms on the outside of the glass, it is ready to drink.

(Continued on next page)

TWIST

Some drinks call for a citrus twist to garnish the cocktail. This is a simple way to make a cocktail look elegant while also adding citrus notes to the aroma of the drink. Use a Y-shaped peeler or sharp paring knife to cut a thin, oval disk out of the citrus peel, avoiding the pith (the white, spongy part). Gently grasp the outer edges skin-side down between your thumb and index and middle fingers and pinch the twist over the drink. Rub the peel around the rim of the glass, then drop it into the drink.

Guide to Glassware

Champagne Flute
This tall tulip-shaped glass is designed to show off the magical bubbles of Champagne as they burst against the glass. It's great for any cocktail made with sparkling wine.

Collins Glass
These tall, narrow glasses originally got their name from the Tom Collins cocktail but are now commonly used for a vast array of mixed drinks.

Coupe Glass
This saucer-shaped stemmed glass, rumored to have originally been designed after the shape of Marie Antoinette's breast, is traditionally used for serving champagne. However, the wide mouth is not great for containing bubbles and is now more commonly used for cocktails without ice.

Glass Goblet
These large tulip-shaped glasses with a short stem are designed for brandy and cognac. The large bowl shape allows for optimal air intake to bring out the flavors of the alcohol.

Glass Tankard (Stein)
This traditional glass beer mug has origins leading back to medieval Germany. Perfect for serving up a drink at any castle feast.

Hurricane Glass
A tall, elegantly cut glass named after its hurricane lamp-like shape, it's often used for exotic/tropical drinks.

(Continued on next page)

Martini Glass

As the name might suggest, this glass is designed with a particular cocktail in mind. These V-shaped long stem glasses are used for a wide range of cocktails served straight up (without ice).

Pint Glass

The pint glass is a staple of any British pub and is designed for the serving of beer and cider. This glassware is designed to hold a British imperial measurement of a pint: 20 oz./568 milliliters. Under British law, it is actually illegal to sell beer in any other glass, as consumer rights dictate that when ordering a pint of beer, it's imperative that a customer gets exactly that!

Rocks Glass

This old-fashioned glass is a short tumbler with a wide base and top, typically associated with whiskey cocktails. The glass was designed to withstand muddling and hold large cubes of ice.

Shot Glass

Used for "shooting" a drink, these small glasses are used for a straight pour of spirits.

Wine Glass

Wine glasses are not just for wine. They can also be used for wine-based cocktails such as wine spritzer.

Novelty Glassware

Cauldron

Perhaps not everyone's first thought for how to serve up cocktails but, for a magic-themed party, a cauldron is a must-have! A large plastic cauldron acts as the perfect punch bowl, and an added sprinkle of dry ice will impress all your friends.

Glass Beaker and Test Tube Shooter

For the serious witches and wizards out there, this is the ultimate way to serve up all your delicious cocktail concoctions. This scientific aesthetic will definitely make you the star of potions class!

Mason Jar

These large square jars, originally designed for preserving fruits and vegetables, have recently become the hip vessel for serving cocktails. With the added bonus that you can pop a lid on top, and take these jarred cocktails with you wherever you go!

Mug

Putting the mug in "muggle," this drinkware basic is perfect for those warm coffee cocktails. Cold cocktails such as the Moscow Mule are traditionally served in copper mugs, as this helps reduce the temperature of the drink.

Teacup

During the 1920s, alcohol was served in teacups as a sneaky way to get around prohibition laws. Now, it's back on trend and looks super Instagrammable (so get your grandma's china at the ready for some gorgeous creations)!

Ingredients

Butterfly Pea Flower Extract

Available online (we recommend b'Lure flower extract) and in certain kitchen supply stores, this relatively unknown ingredient will turn drinks from blue to purple and then pink with only a few drops! Used in traditional medicine and as a natural food coloring throughout Asia, this unique ingredient acts as a natural litmus test, changing color with the acidity of a drink. Top off potions with this truly magical ingredient!

Citrus Juice

Lemon, lime, or grapefruit juice can be found in the vast majority of cocktails. It is always preferable to use freshly squeezed citrus juice when making a cocktail.

Edible Glitter

Edible drink glitter is now widely available in a variety of colors and flavors and is a great way to turn an ordinary cocktail into an extraordinary one. When in doubt, add glitter and prepare to be enchanted!

Eggs

A few cocktails in this book call for egg whites and yolks. However, if you are vegan, aquafaba (the water from chickpeas) can be used as a substitute for egg whites.

Flavored Syrup

Syrups are commercially available to purchase in many different flavors and are a simple way to add a new twist to a cocktail. For those who pride themselves on their potion-making ability (and want to save a few pennies), they are also simple enough to make at home (recipes on pages 12–14).

INFUSED ALCOHOL

Flavors can easily be added to alcohols like vodka. This is the main principle behind the Every Flavor Jelly Shots (page 93) and can be applied to larger quantities and many different flavors. You can really experiment with infusing using fruits and herbs, so be creative and find what tastes best to you!

SPECIAL INGREDIENTS

Some of the recipes in this book call for special ingredients to recreate real-life wizarding magic: baking soda, activated charcoal, citric acid, sodium alginate, and calcium lactate. All sound as though they come straight out of a chemistry textbook, but it is important to purchase these ingredients at a high enough purity for human consumption.

Homemade Syrups

Custom cocktail syrups are one of those special ingredients that can magically transform a drink. Whether it's basic simple syrup, a seasonal flavor combination such as cinnamon syrup, or something fruity like passion fruit syrup, you can easily make it and enjoy it at home! Remember to take care and use sensible safety measures when working with heated sugar.

Simple Syrup

Sometimes referred to as sugar syrup, this simple-to-create cocktail staple is basically a supersaturated mixture of sugar and water. The most common version uses two parts sugar to one part water (2:1). To make it, add the sugar and water to a saucepan and heat at a medium temperature until all the sugar is dissolved. Then, take off the heat and allow to cool. Simple syrup can be stored for up to 1 month in the fridge.

Honey Syrup

Honey syrup is easy to make; combine equal parts honey with water in a saucepan, heat until dissolved (no more than a minute), then cool to room temperature before using.

Caramel Syrup

- 1 cup (200 grams) sugar
- ½ cup (130 milliliters) water, divided
- 1 teaspoon pure vanilla extract
- pinch salt

In a small saucepan over low heat, combine the sugar and ¼ cup (60 milliliters) water. Stir constantly until the sugar dissolves, 8 to 10 minutes. Turn up the heat to medium-high, cover, and boil for 3 minutes. Remove from heat. Add the remaining water in a slow stream, stirring constantly. Stir in the vanilla extract and salt. Let the syrup cool completely, then transfer to a sealed container and store in the refrigerator for up to 1 month.

Passion Fruit Syrup
- ½ cup (100 grams) sugar
- ½ cup (130 milliliters) water
- 4 ripe passion fruits

In a small saucepan over low heat, combine the sugar and water. Stir occasionally until the sugar has completely dissolved, then remove from heat. Slice passion fruits in half and scoop out the pulp into the simple syrup. Let the fruit steep in the syrup for 2 hours. Pour the solution through a fine mesh sieve into a glass storage container with a lid. To avoid a cloudy simple syrup, don't press on the solids; let the syrup drain naturally. Store the syrup in the refrigerator for up to 1 month.

Cinnamon Syrup
- ½ cup (100 grams) sugar
- ½ cup (130 milliliters) water
- 6 cinnamon sticks

In a small saucepan over low heat, combine the sugar and water. Stir occasionally until the sugar has completely dissolved, then remove from heat. Drop cinnamon sticks into the simple syrup, cover, and let the mixture sit overnight. Then, remove the cinnamon sticks and store syrup in a glass container with a lid for up to two weeks.

Ginger Syrup
- ½ cup (100 grams) sugar
- ⅓ cup (80 milliliters) water
- ½ cup (45 grams) fresh ginger root, peeled and sliced

In a saucepan on medium heat, combine the sugar and water. Stir constantly until the sugar is dissolved. Add the ginger and continue to heat, bringing the syrup to a light boil. Cover, reduce heat, and allow to simmer for 15 minutes. Remove from heat, allow to cool, and steep in the covered pan for about 1 hour. The ginger syrup can be stored in the refrigerator for up to 1 month.

(Continued on next page)

Strawberry Syrup

- ⅓ pound (130 grams) strawberries
- ½ cup (130 milliliters) water
- ⅓ cup (65 grams) sugar

Rinse the strawberries, remove the stems, and slice them into smaller pieces. Place the strawberry slices in a saucepan, cover with water, and slowly bring to a boil. Reduce to a simmer and let the strawberries cook for approximately 20 minutes or until the strawberries lose most of their color and the water turns deep pink or red in color. Remove from heat, strain the strawberry liquid through a fine mesh sieve into another clean pot to separate the solid berries from the liquid, and discard the solid berries. Add the sugar to the strawberry liquid. Bring to a boil, stirring frequently to dissolve the sugar into the syrup. Let the syrup simmer for 5 minutes until the sugar is completely dissolved. Remove the syrup from the heat and allow it to cool completely. Pour into a glass container, seal, and refrigerate for up to 1 month.

GARNISHES

CITRUS
The most widely used garnishes are citrus fruits. Whether a cocktail calls for a citrus wheel (thin, circular cross-section), a wedge, or the more elegant twist, these garnishes don't just look fantastic, they also add aroma and flavor.

EDIBLE FLOWERS
Flowers bring a fresh botanical touch to many cocktails (as well as being picture perfect) and can be purchased online and at certain supermarkets or cake decorating supply stores. The most commonly used edible flowers in cocktail making are cornflowers, nasturtium, pansies, lavender, dandelions, and violets.

FRUIT
Many exotic cocktails call for fruit garnish such as pineapple, cherries, and strawberries, to name a few. Either cut the fruit into wedges or use a cocktail stick to skewer the fruit and lay it on top of the glass.

INEDIBLE FLOURISHES
A tiny cocktail umbrella, once the height of sophistication, can now look a bit outdated. But don't let this stop you from playing around with some other wacky flourishes. Whether using wands as cocktail stirrers, or dropping in a few fake spiders, the sky's the limit with what you can create. However, all good witches and wizards know to ditch the plastic straws in favor of reusable or eco-friendly!

(Continued on next page)

Herbs

Herb garnishes are often used in cocktail making. Mint is most frequently used in this book, as it not only looks pretty but adds a sweet refreshing aroma as well. To ace herbology, place the leaves flat between your palms and clap to really release their essential oils before placing them in your drink.

Savory Garnishes

A few cocktails in this book such as Bloodier than Mary (page 81) and Loose-Lipped Libation (page 116) call for savory garnishes like celery and olives. This is arguably one of the best ways to get your five-a-day.

Elf and Safety

Cocktail making is not all fun and games, so read these educational decrees and use all necessary protective spells and equipment to ensure everyone has a good time:

Activated Charcoal Powder (a.k.a. Peruvian Instant Darkness Powder)

Activated charcoal powder can be purchased in many health food stores. It has a long history of being used as a detoxifying agent and can dramatically change the appearance of a cocktail. However, it can be problematic if mixed with certain medication, so we recommend avoiding consuming cocktails containing charcoal if you are taking any medicine, contraceptive pills, or vitamin supplements.

Dry Ice Pellets

Dry ice is the common name for solid carbon dioxide. It is appearing in more and more cocktails and can be ordered relatively easily online, but dry ice does not stay solid forever, so timing is key.

Dry ice begins to sublimate at -108°F (-78°C), therefore care must be taken when handling. Gloves should always be worn when handling dry ice to make sure that there is no contact with bare skin. It is also essential to only use dry ice in a well-ventilated area.

For cocktail making, dry ice pellets work best, as this allows you to only add as needed (typically 2–3 pellets per cocktail). The pellets will quickly dissolve to create a smoky/foggy effect. Take care when adding dry ice pellets to a drink; the drink will often fizz over if you add too many too quickly.

Most important, *never* consume a dry ice pellet, as this can lead to some serious health problems. Always wait for the smoky/foggy effect to finish before taking your first sip.

(Continued on next page)

IGNITION

Setting cocktails on fire is the quintessential party trick. While the fire enriches the flavor of the alcohol, it is also the perfect way to entertain guests. High-proof spirits like overproof rum are perfect for igniting at room temperature. Because of the high proof of the spirit, you can "top" a drink with the alcohol (being careful not to mix it). This is best done by pouring the high-proof alcohol across the back of a spoon touching the side of the glass.

Apply a flame to the spirit, making sure to keep your hands and any other flammable material out of the way. Be prepared to yell "Incendio!" and wow your friends with this spectacularly magical flamed party trick.

SPARKLERS

To add an extra "wow" factor to your cocktails, try indoor mini sparklers. Always light away from flammable material and wait until the sparkler is fully extinguished before taking a sip! Be prepared to watch the sparks fly and impress your friends.

Part II

Magical Cocktails

All cocktails approved by the Department of Intoxicating Substances
for wizards and witches of drinking age.

ESSENTIAL ELIXIRS

Butterscotch Beer

This student favorite will warm your bones and transport you straight into the magical realm.
Serve in a glass tankard to get the full effect and picture yourself in front of a roaring fire at
your magical haunt of choice.

Serves: *1*
Preparation time: *15 minutes*
Glassware: *Glass tankard*

3 ounces
  (90 milliliters)
  apple cider
1 ounce (30 milliliters)
  Scotch whisky
1–3 tablespoons
  butterscotch sauce
1½ ounces
  (60 milliliters)
  ginger beer
Garnish: whipped cream

◆ In a saucepan, gently heat the apple cider, Scotch, and butterscotch until the sauce is fully dissolved and the mixture is steaming but not boiling, 5 to 10 minutes. Remove from heat and stir in the ginger beer. Ladle into a glass tankard and garnish with whipped cream.

Great Ball of Fire

This cocktail is a true showstopper and will leave your guests in awe. Get ready to shout "Incendio!" and watch the pale blue flames flicker. By carefully garnishing with cinnamon, you can conjure up a delicious aroma, and when the fire dies out, this cocktail will not disappoint.

Serves: *1*
Preparation time: *5 minutes*
Glassware: *Glass goblet*

2 ounces (60 milliliters) vodka

2 ounces (60 milliliters) blue curaçao

4 ounces (120 milliliters) lemonade

⅕ ounce (6 milliliters) overproof rum

Garnish: ground cinnamon

◆ Pour the vodka, blue curaçao, and lemonade into a glass goblet and give a gentle stir. Carefully add the overproof rum to the surface of the drink and ignite.* Sprinkle cinnamon onto the flames. Remember, do not consume the cocktail until the flame is out.

---

*See Elf and Safety on page 18 for instructions on how to ignite a cocktail.

Botanical Cocktail

This botanical cocktail is a must for all plant lovers out there. This simple recipe is foolproof to brew, so you don't need to be an expert in herbology to enjoy this one.

Serves: 1
Preparation time: 5 minutes
Glassware: Collins glass

2 teaspoons sugar

1 stalk lemongrass, small-chopped

1 cucumber

1 ounce (30 milliliters) fresh lime juice

6–8 mint leaves

2 ounces (60 milliliters) light rum

ice cubes

chilled soda water, to top glass

Garnish: mint sprig

◆ Add the sugar and lemongrass into a glass and, using a muddler, mash the ingredients together. Next, using a spiralizer or vegetable peeler, grate the skin off the cucumber and add it to the glass. Combine the fresh lime juice with the mint leaves and muddle the concoction again. Then, pour in the rum and ice and give the mixture a stir. Top the glass with chilled soda water and garnish with a mint sprig.

Fire Whiskey

A shot of this cocktail is a surefire way to cure any resting witch face! Don't hesitate to add some fire to your night and enjoy the warming sensation of this powerful little cocktail.

Serves: 1
Preparation time: 3 minutes
Glassware: Rocks glass

1 ounce (30 milliliters) bourbon whiskey

½ ounce (15 milliliters) cinnamon schnapps

ice cubes

1 teaspoon overproof rum

◆ Combine the whiskey and cinnamon schnapps in a cocktail shaker with a handful of ice cubes. Shake vigorously until the mixture is cool. Strain into a rocks glass, top with overproof rum, and ignite.* Remember, do not consume the cocktail until the flame is out.

---

*See Elf and Safety on page 18 for instructions on how to ignite a cocktail.

Spiced Pumpkin Juice

This charming cocktail has always been extremely popular in the wizarding world and is the perfect indulgence for those long autumnal nights. Whether serving at a Halloween bash or simply to enjoy by yourself while reading a good book, this martini never misses the mark.

Serves: 1
Preparation time: 5 minutes
Glassware: Martini glass

2 tablespoons caramel syrup (recipe on page 12), to rim glass
pinch cinnamon-sugar
ice cubes
1 ounce (30 milliliters) cinnamon whiskey
1 ounce (30 milliliters) pumpkin spice liqueur
1½ ounces (45 milliliters) Irish cream
1 ounce (30 milliliters) simple syrup (recipe on page 12)
Garnish: whipped cream

◆ Rim the edge of a martini glass with caramel syrup and cinnamon-sugar (learn how to rim a glass on page 5). In a cocktail shaker, add the ice, whiskey, pumpkin spice liqueur, Irish cream, and simple syrup. Shake the ingredients thoroughly until chilled. Strain the mixture into the rimmed glass and top with whipped cream.

Elf-Made Wine

This summer berry red wine spritzer is a cool and refreshing cocktail. Full of strawberries and blueberries, it's perfect for times when you want to stay away from the hard stuff. However, it is still strong enough to get a house elf or two tipsy!

Serves: 1
Preparation time: 5 minutes
Glassware: Wine glass

ice cubes

2–3 strawberries

4–5 blueberries

½ teaspoon honey

1 ounce (15 milliliters) fresh lime juice

4 ounces (120 milliliters) red wine

1¾ ounces (50 milliliters) soda water

Garnish: mint sprig

◆ Fill a wine glass with a handful of ice cubes along with the strawberries and blueberries. Next add the honey and lime juice and give everything a good mix. To finish the spritzer, combine the wine and soda water. Garnish with a mint sprig.

Classic Concoctions

Cobweb under the Stairs

Dust away the cobwebs with this sparkly little number that is sure to lift the spirits. A spin on classic summer flavors, this cocktail is ideal for sitting and sipping in the garden while dreaming of escaping on a magical adventure.

Serves: 1
Preparation time: 20 minutes
Glassware: Wine glass

Garnish: spun sugar cobwebs
ice cubes
⅞ ounce (25 milliliters) gin
⅔ ounce (20 milliliters) elderflower liqueur
⅞ ounce (25 milliliters) lemon juice
2⅗ ounces (75 milliliters) prosecco
pinch edible glitter (preferably silver or iridescent)

◆ First, prepare your spun sugar cobwebs (recipe below). Then, add a handful of ice cubes to a cocktail shaker and add the gin, elderflower liqueur, and lemon juice. Shake until cool and strain into the wine glass. Top with prosecco. Nestle the spun sugar cobwebs onto the top of the glass and sprinkle with edible glitter.

Spun Sugar Cobwebs

⅔ cup (128 grams) granulated sugar
1 tablespoon water

◆ Set out a couple of baking sheets on a work surface so that they cover the area you will be working in and place a large mixing bowl in the center. Remember to take sensible precautions when working with heated sugar.

(Continued on next page)

◆ Combine the water and sugar in a small steel saucepan, making sure the sugar is distributed evenly over the bottom of the pan. Place on medium-high heat until all the sugar is dissolved and the syrup is just beginning to turn a pale golden color. It is important *not* to stir the sugar during this time, otherwise the sugar may crystallize.

◆ Remove the pan from the heat and set aside on a heat-proof surface to cool until the syrup forms thin threads (rather than droplets) when dipping a fork in and lifting.

◆ When the syrup is ready, dip the fork into the syrup and fling sugar threads quickly back and forth across the large mixing bowl, moving the fork up and down and all around to form gossamer threads.

◆ Repeat until you have formed a web, then let the sugar cool for a few seconds. Starting from the bottom, quickly ease the threads out of the bowl and shape into a loose sphere with your fork. Using a new fork for each web, repeat as many times as needed.

The Sophisticated Sour

The Sophisticated Sour is the most exclusive cocktail in the wizarding world. This recipe has been carefully cultivated to ensure that each ingredient is the best of the best. Those who are naturally talented at mixology will reap the benefits of this sophisticated, smooth, and fruity delight.

Serves: 1
Preparation time: 10 minutes
Glassware: Coupe glass

⁴/₅ ounce
  (25 milliliters)
  raspberry cordial
1¾ ounces
  (50 milliliters) gin
⁴/₅ ounce
  (25 milliliters) fresh
  lemon juice
1 tablespoon egg white
ice cubes
Garnish: 3 fresh
  raspberries on a
  cocktail stick

For the Cocktail

◆ First, make the raspberry cordial (recipe below). In a cocktail shaker, combine the raspberry cordial, gin, lemon juice, and the egg white in a cocktail shaker and shake for one minute to froth the egg white. Next, add a handful of ice cubes to the shaker and shake until cool. Strain the cocktail into a coupe glass and garnish with fresh raspberries on a cocktail stick.

For the Raspberry Cordial

4 ounces (120 grams) fresh raspberries
2½ ounces (75 milliliters) water
2½ ounces (75 grams) demerara sugar
zest of 1 lemon

◆ Combine the ingredients in a pan and simmer on medium heat until the raspberries start to break up. Remove the pan from the heat and allow to cool. Once cool, strain through a fine sieve. The raspberry cordial can be stored in a sterilized bottle and kept refrigerated for up to 1 month.

Unicorn's Blood

It has been said that unicorn blood will keep you alive even if you are an inch from death, but at a terrible price . . . but we promise the hangover will be worth it for this delicious shimmering cocktail.

Serves: 1
Preparation time: 5 minutes
Glassware: Martini glass

1½ ounces
(45 milliliters) gin
1½ ounces
(45 milliliters)
elderflower
liqueur
1 ounce (30 milliliters)
fresh lemon juice
pinch edible glitter
ice cubes

◆ Combine the gin, elderflower liqueur, lemon juice, and edible glitter in a cocktail shaker with a handful of ice cubes. Shake until cool and strain into a martini glass.

Phoenix Song

This colorful cocktail will help you rise from the ashes to find your second wind, while hitting all the right notes. For that extra flare, add an indoor miniature sparkler to make it truly magical.

Serves: 1
Preparation time: 5 minutes
Glassware: Hurricane glass

2 tablespoons grenadine

1¾ ounces (50 milliliters) tequila

1 ounce (30 milliliters) triple sec

1 ounce (30 milliliters) fresh lemon juice

1 teaspoon orange juice

ice cubes

Garnish: orange wedge, indoor miniature sparkler, and strawberry

◆ Pour the grenadine into the base of a hurricane glass and set aside. In a cocktail shaker, combine the tequila, triple sec, and fruit juices with a handful of ice cubes. Shake until the mixture is cool. Being careful not to disturb the grenadine layer, add the ice cubes to the hurricane glass and strain the cocktail (learn how to layer ingredients on page 5). Add more ice to fill the glass and garnish with an orange wedge. For the final flourish, secure an indoor miniature sparkler in a strawberry and light before serving (see Elf and Safety on page 18 for instructions on how to safely use sparklers). Remove and safely dispose of the spent sparkler before drinking.

Smokey Dragon's Breath

A smokey sensation to give the vibe of brooding brimstone and cold winter nights spent in castle towers, this cocktail is a vaporous vision that tastes as good as it looks. Be ready to battle fire and flame as you mix these fierce flavors.

Serves: 1
Preparation time: 15 minutes
Glassware: Large re-sealable glass bottle, glass jug, and a rocks glass

1 stick apple wood, to produce smoke

sugar cube

2 dashes (2 milliliters) orange bitters

1¾ ounces (50 milliliters) peated Scotch whisky

ice cubes

Garnish: orange twist

◆ Start with an uncluttered surface that is free of anything flammable. A large wooden chopping board is ideal for this. Have your large re-sealable glass bottle open and close at hand. Use a lighter to light the stick of apple wood, turning it in the flame until it begins to ignite. As soon as it begins to catch, blow out the flame so that the applewood is smoking, incense-style. Set it down on the chopping board so that the stick is balancing on its end. Immediately place your open glass bottle over the top and let it fill with smoke until the glass turns opaque, then lift off the bottle and immediately seal. Set to one side. Place the smoking applewood in a cup of water to make sure it is safely extinguished.

◆ Next, place a sugar cube in a glass jug. Add the bitters and muddle. Pour in the Scotch. Open your bottle of smoke and immediately pour in the contents of the jug using a strainer. Seal once more. Ensure your bottle is fully sealed, then shake. The more you shake the bottle, the smokier the cocktail will be. Set to one side.

◆ Add ice cubes to a rocks glass. Open the bottle and pour out the smoking cocktail. Garnish with an orange twist. Sit and sip your smoking sensation.

Knight-Cap Bus

Let this vividly purple cocktail take you on a magical journey! With no ticket necessary, this is a favorite for many witches and wizards on the move. Hold on tight, don't misplace any luggage, and trust that this cocktail will get you where you need to go!

Serves: 1
Preparation time: 5 minutes
Glassware: Rocks glass

1 ounce (30 milliliters)
   blue curaçao
1½ ounces
   (45 milliliters)
   vodka
1 ounce (30 milliliters)
   cranberry juice
ice cubes
Garnish: viola flower
   or any other edible
   purple flower

◆ Combine the blue curaçao, vodka, and cranberry juice in a cocktail shaker with a handful of ice cubes. Shake until cool and strain into a rocks glass. Garnish with an edible purple flower.

Red Hot Letter

Delivering a strong message (and flavor), this drink is definitely difficult to ignore—and something to shout about! Be prepared to add some spice to your night with this fiery little cocktail.

Serves: *1*
Preparation time: *5 minutes*
Glassware: *Rocks glass*

½ ounce
   (15 milliliters) agave
   nectar

1 chili pepper, sliced

3 lime wedges

2 ounces
   (60 milliliters)
   cachaça

pinch salt

1 ounce (30 milliliters)
   lime juice

crushed ice

Garnish: sliced chili
   pepper and lime
   wedge

◆ In a cocktail shaker, combine the agave, sliced chili pepper, and lime wedges and muddle. Next, add in the cachaça, salt, and lime juice along with a handful of crushed ice. Shake until cool and pour (unstrained) into a rocks glass. Garnish with an additional slice of chili pepper and a lime wedge.

Hair of
the Dog

Rumored to cure even the sorest of heads, there is no excuse not to keep the party going when you can summon up this blue and boozy cocktail.

Serves: *1*
Preparation time: *5 minutes*
Glassware: *Hurricane glass*

crushed ice

1 ounce (30 milliliters) blue curaçao

1 ounce (30 milliliters) vodka

Lemonade, to top glass

Garnish: 3 maraschino cherries on a skewer

◆ Fill a hurricane glass with crushed ice and add the blue curaçao and vodka. Top with lemonade and garnish with three maraschino cherries on a skewer.

Honey-Mead Station

*Get on board with this delicious drink's perfect blend of sweet honey and bitter orange flavors.
See where the night takes you with this first-class cocktail!*

Serves: 1
Preparation time: 10 minutes
Glassware: Rocks glass

3 blackberries

2 tablespoons honey
   syrup (recipe on
   page 12)

2 dashes (2 milliliters)
   angostura bitters

orange twist

large ice cube

1½ ounces
   (45 milliliters) mead

1 ounce (30 milliliters)
   bourbon whiskey

⅕ ounce (6 milliliters)
   water

◆ Combine the blackberries, honey
syrup, bitters, and orange twist in a rocks
glass. Muddle the ingredients, bursting
the blackberries, then add a single
large ice cube, followed by the mead,
bourbon, and water. Using a bar spoon,
gently stir the mixture.

The Prophecy

This silky smooth drink is not only a legend but also a must-try for all cocktail lovers! Make this your chosen drink of the night and see if you live to tell the tale.

Serves: *1*
Preparation time: *5 minutes*
Glassware: *Rocks glass*

2 ounces
(60 milliliters)
bourbon whiskey

1 ounce (30 milliliters)
fresh lemon juice

½ ounce
(15 milliliters)
simple syrup (recipe
on page 12)

2 dashes (2 milliliters)
angostura bitters

½ fresh egg white

ice cubes

crushed ice

Garnish: orange wedge
and a cherry

◆ In a cocktail shaker, combine the bourbon, lemon juice, simple syrup, bitters, and egg white with a handful of ice cubes and shake until chilled. Strain over crushed ice in a rocks glass. Garnish with an orange wedge and a cherry.

Disappearing Daiquiri

This cocktail is a firm favorite and gives a real pop of fun to any celebration. Simple to prepare and so delicious, this drink never hangs around for long! Send shooting stars, as well as your guests, dancing around the living room with this Disappearing Daiquiri.

Serves: 1
Preparation time: 5 minutes
Glassware: Coupe glass

1 packet popping
    candy, to rim glass
1¾ ounces
    (50 milliliters) light
    rum
⅞ ounce
    (25 milliliters)
    simple syrup (recipe
    on page 12)
⅞ ounce
    (25 milliliters) fresh
    lime juice
ice cubes
Garnish: lime wheel,
    whole strawberry,
    and a miniature
    sparkler

◆ Rim a coupe glass with popping candy (learn how to rim a glass on page 5). In a cocktail shaker, add the rum, simple syrup, lime juice, and ice cubes. Shake until cool and strain into the rimmed glass. Garnish with a wheel of lime and a whole strawberry. For the final flourish, secure a miniature sparkler in a strawberry and light before serving (see Elf and Safety on page 18 for instructions on how to safely use sparklers). Remove and safely dispose of the spent sparkler before drinking.

CHARMING COCKTAILS

Killer Piña Colada

Want to kill it at your next party? Then this unforgivable cocktail is a must-have! The melon liqueur gives this drink a sinister green tint as well as making it fruity, refreshing, and truly deadly.

Serves: *1*
Preparation time: *5 minutes*
Glassware: *Hurricane glass*

4 ounces
  (120 milliliters)
  pineapple juice

2 ounces
  (60 milliliters)
  melon liqueur

1 ounce (30 milliliters)
  light rum

2 ounces
  (60 milliliters)
  coconut cream

ice cubes

Garnish: pineapple slice

◆ In a blender, combine the pineapple juice, melon liqueur, rum, coconut cream, and a handful of ice cubes. Blend until smooth. Serve in a hurricane glass and garnish with a slice of pineapple.

Magic Martini

This reboot of the classic espresso martini is the perfect nighttime pick-me-up guaranteed to keep you dancing well beyond the witching hour. Try switching to decaffeinated coffee if the Undesirable No. 1 side effect is getting too much of a buzz!

Serves: 1
Preparation time: 5 minutes
Glassware: Martini glass

2 ounces
   (60 milliliters)
   vodka
1¾ ounces
   (50 milliliters)
   coffee liqueur
1¾ ounces
   (50 milliliters)
   chilled espresso
ice cubes
Garnish: 2–3 coffee
   beans

◆ In a cocktail shaker, combine the vodka, coffee liqueur, and espresso with a handful of ice cubes and shake until cool. Strain and serve in a martini glass. Garnish with 2 to 3 coffee beans.

Color-Changing Charm

This charming color-changing cocktail is a real people pleaser! Elate your guests by using some old-fashioned science magic to turn this concoction from blue to pink—as if by the wave of a wand!

Serves: 1
Preparation time: 5 minutes
Glassware: Coupe glass and shot glass

2 tablespoons salt, to rim glass

1¾ ounces (50 milliliters) tequila

⅞ ounce (25 milliliters) triple sec

2–3 tablespoons butterfly pea flower extract

pinch edible glitter

ice cubes

⅞ ounce (25 milliliters) fresh lemon juice

◆ Rim a coupe glass with salt (learn how to rim a glass on page 5). In a cocktail shaker, combine the tequila, triple sec, butterfly pea flower extract, and a pinch of edible glitter along with a handful of ice cubes. Shake until cool and strain into the rimmed coupe glass. Next, squeeze the fresh lemon juice into a shot glass and, only when you want to show off the cocktail's color-changing properties, pour it in. (The butterfly pea flower extract works as a natural pH indicator and will react to the increase in acidity from the lemon juice by changing the color of the drink!)

Obliterate

This seriously strong cocktail is as good as any memory charm in making you forget all your misdeeds and adventures the next morning! Relax and let this enchanting cocktail work its magic.

Serves: *1*
Preparation time: *5 minutes*
Glassware: *Coupe glass*

¾ ounce
(22 milliliters) gin

¾ ounce
(22 milliliters) Lillet Blanc

¾ ounce
(22 milliliters) triple sec

¾ ounce
(22 milliliters) fresh lime juice

ice cubes

absinthe, to top glass

Garnish: lemon twist

◆ In a cocktail shaker, combine the gin, Lillet Blanc, triple sec, and lime juice with a handful of ice cubes. Shake until cold, then strain into a coupe glass. Top with absinthe and garnish with a lemon twist.

Hex on the Beach

Based on the classic, this eye-catching cocktail completes any young witch's night out. Be prepared to dream about the sand between your toes and apparating to your next holiday with this tropical and refreshing cocktail.

Serves: *1*
Preparation time: *5 minutes*
Glassware: *Hurricane glass*

ice cubes

1½ ounce
   (45 milliliters)
   vodka

½ ounce
   (15 milliliters) peach
   liqueur

2 ounces
   (60 milliliters) no-
   pulp orange juice

2 ounces
   (60 milliliters)
   cranberry juice

Garnish: lime wheel,
   maraschino cherry,
   and pinch edible
   glitter

◆ Fill a hurricane glass with ice cubes and gently layer in the vodka, peach liqueur, and orange and cranberry juices to achieve an orange-to-red ombré effect (learn how to layer ingredients on page 5). Top with a lime wheel, cherry, and a pinch of edible glitter to really give it a magical effect.

CHARACTERFUL CREATIONS

Mysterious Tea

Making this mysterious cocktail can be an inexact science, but if you're a natural your efforts will be rewarded with this deliciously divine drink. Once consumed, be sure to read the mint leaves and predict your future. Who knows what the night might hold!

Serves: *1*
Preparation time: *10 minutes*
Glassware: *Teacup and saucer*

8 ounces
    (240 milliliters)
    black tea

1 tablespoon sugar

2 slices lemon

mint leaves

crushed ice

1½ ounces
    (45 milliliters)
    sherry

½ ounce
    (15 milliliters) triple
    sec

Garnish: mint sprig and
    edible flower

◆ Make the black tea in a heat-proof jug and mix in the sugar. Allow the solution to cool to room temperature. In a teacup, use a muddler to gently grind the sliced lemon and mint leaves to release their flavor. Add a handful of crushed ice and pour in the sherry and triple sec. Top with the cooled tea. Add a mint spring and an edible flower to garnish.

Speeding Sidecar

Buckle up as this drink hits some real heights with its mix of cognac and triple sec, making for quite a strong cocktail. It's enough to put hair on your chest!

Serves: 1
Preparation time: 5 minutes
Glassware: Coupe glass

2 ounces
(60 milliliters)
cognac

1 ounce (30 milliliters)
triple sec

1 ounce (30 milliliters)
fresh lemon juice

1 teaspoon simple
syrup (recipe on
page 12)

ice cubes

Garnish: orange wedge

◆ In a cocktail shaker, combine the cognac, triple sec, lemon juice, and simple syrup with a handful of ice cubes. Shake until the mixture is cool. Strain into a coupe glass and garnish with an orange wedge.

Gin-Fizz-Bangs

For all those who solemnly swear they are up to no good . . . this is the perfect cocktail for you!
Create an explosion of excitement with these Aperol-flavored cocktail bombs. Simple to make,
when added to the clear cocktail they fizz and transform to create a new color and flavor!

Serves: 6
Preparation time: 1-2 hours
Glassware: Wine glass

For the Cocktail Bomb

1 tablespoon baking soda
1 tablespoon Aperol
2 teaspoons orange concentrate
1 teaspoon orange food coloring
2¼ ounces (64 grams) icing sugar
2¼ ounces (64 grams) caster sugar
1½ tablespoons citric acid
pinch edible glitter
bath bomb mold

For the Cocktail (per serving)

2 ounces (60 milliliters) gin
1 ounce (30 milliliters) fresh
  lemon juice
1 ounce (30 milliliters) simple
  syrup (recipe on page 12)
ice cubes
lemonade, to top glass
Garnish: sliced cucumber

◆ For the cocktail bomb, mix together the baking soda, Aperol, and orange concentrate and food coloring, working quickly to get rid of any big lumps. Add in the icing sugar, caster sugar, citric acid, and edible glitter and mix well. Press into the bath molds, then leave to dry out for an hour or two.

◆ For the cocktail, in a cocktail shaker combine the gin, lemon juice, and simple syrup with a handful of ice cubes. Shake until cool and strain into a wine glass. Top with lemonade and garnish with sliced cucumber. Upon serving, add one of the cocktail bombs and watch it fizz and transform into an Aperol-infused cocktail.

Victor Rum

This champion of cocktails is a great combination of tropical rums and flavors. The perfect accompaniment to relaxing and enjoying some world-class sporting tournaments on a hot summer's day.

Serves: 1
Preparation time: 5 minutes
Glassware: Tankard

2 ounces
   (60 milliliters) gold
   rum
½ ounce
   (15 milliliters)
   coconut rum
2 ounces
   (60 milliliters)
   pineapple juice
½ ounce
   (15 milliliters)
   passion fruit syrup
   (recipe on page 13)
½ ounce
   (15 milliliters) fresh
   lime juice
ice cubes
crushed ice
Garnish: pineapple
   wedge

◆ In a cocktail shaker, combine the gold and coconut rums, pineapple juice, passion fruit syrup, and lime juice with a handful of ice cubes. Shake vigorously until the contents are cool. Strain into a tankard over crushed ice and garnish with a pineapple wedge.

Pimm's O'clock

All hands point to relax on the family clock when Molly sits down to enjoy a refreshing glass of Pimm's. When she's not busy knitting jumpers or battling the forces of darkness, Molly is very partial to enjoying some downtime with this oh–so–British cocktail. Sit back, relax, and imagine you're sipping this summery treat in the garden. Just be on the lookout for any biting gnomes!

Serves: *1*
Preparation time: *5 minutes*
Glassware: *Collins glass*

ice cubes
2 ounces
   (60 milliliters)
   Pimm's No. 1
   liqueur
lemonade, to top glass
Garnish: mint sprigs,
   sliced cucumber,
   oranges, and
   strawberries

◆ Add a handful of ice cubes to a collins glass. Pour over the Pimm's and top with lemonade. Garnish with mint sprigs, sliced cucumber, oranges, and strawberries.

Deoch-an-Darkness

This cocktail may look all pink and rosy but, be warned, it has a very dark side! A few sips of the Deoch-an-Darkness can lead to some terrible life choices, whether that is texting an ex, singing some off-key karaoke, or being dragged away by angry centaurs!

Serves: 1
Preparation time: 5 minutes
Glass: Teacup and saucer (cat print optional) or coupe glass

1¾ ounces (50 milliliters) rose- and cucumber-infused gin (see page 11 for instructions on how to infuse alcohol)

¼ ounce (7.5 milliliters) grenadine

½ ounce (15 milliliters) simple syrup (recipe on page 12)

1 dash (1 milliliter) rose water

¼ ounce (7.5 milliliters) fresh lemon juice

¼ ounce (7.5 milliliters) fresh grapefruit juice

ice cubes

Garnish: rose petal

◆ In a cocktail shaker, combine the gin, grenadine, simple syrup, rose water, and lemon and grapefruit juices with a handful of ice cubes and shake until cool. Strain the mixture into a teacup or coupe glass and garnish with a rose petal.

Seriously Blackberry Bramble

This handsome and charming cocktail wants nothing more than to take you on your next crazy adventure. Simply sweet and delicious, this Seriously Blackberry Bramble always leads to an extremely entertaining night!

Serves: 1
Preparation time: 5 minutes
Glassware: Rocks glass

fresh blackberries

2 ounces (60 milliliters) gin

1 ounce (30 milliliters) Crème de Mûre (blackberry liqueur)

1½ ounces (45 milliliters) fresh lemon juice

1 ounce (30 milliliters) simple syrup (recipe on page 12)

ice cubes

Ginger beer, to top glass

Garnish: blackberry on a skewer and lemon zest

◆ In a cocktail shaker, muddle the blackberries with the gin, Crème de Mûre, lemon juice, and simple syrup. Double strain the mixture using a mesh strainer to remove any blackberry seeds. Fill a rocks glass with ice cubes and pour in the strained gin mix. Top with ginger beer and garnish with a blackberry on a skewer and lemon zest.

Sour-Rita

This heady blend of sweet and salty has earned a reputation as Rita Skeeter's drink of choice. Don't be fooled by the sweet taste of the honey syrup, there's a sour kick hidden within which is just as sharp as Rita's Quick-Quotes Quill! Delicious and full of fruity flavors, just be careful that after one of these, you don't end up spilling your secrets—only to find them splashed over the covers of the Daily Prophet!

Serves: 2
Preparation time: 5 minutes
Glassware: Coupe glass

2 tablespoons salt

1 drop green food coloring

1 pink dragon fruit

2 ounces (60 milliliters) fresh lime juice

3 ounces (90 milliliters) tequila

1½ ounces (45 milliliters) honey syrup (recipe on page 12)

ice cubes

◆ In a mortar and pestle, grind the salt with the green food coloring. Rim a coupe glass (learn how to rim a glass on page 5) with the green salt. Slice the dragon fruit in half and scoop out the flesh with a spoon. In a blender, combine the flesh of the dragon fruit with the lime juice, tequila, honey syrup, and ice. Blend until smooth and serve in the salt-rimmed coupe glass.

Misleading Mudslide

The Misleading Mudslide is a truly indulgent dessert disguised as a cocktail. But this is not a loyal cocktail; it will betray you at the last minute and leave you with a tremendous headache if you are not careful!

Serves: 1
Preparation time: 5 minutes
Glassware: Coupe glass

1 ounce (30 milliliters) vodka

1 ounce (30 milliliters) coffee liqueur

1 ounce (30 milliliters) Irish cream

1½ ounces (45 milliliters) heavy cream

ice cubes

Garnish: chocolate shavings

◆ In a cocktail shaker, combine the vodka, coffee liqueur, Irish cream, and heavy cream with a handful of ice cubes and shake until cool. Strain into a coupe glass and garnish with chocolate shavings.

Tom Collins

This infamous cocktail is perhaps one of the greatest and most well-known drinks to have ever been served! Although the popularity of the Tom Collins has dwindled in recent years, it still commands a loyal following of devoted fans who believe that this cocktail is destined to rise to power again.

Serves: 1
Preparation time: 5 minutes
Glassware: Collins glass

ice cubes

2 ounces
(60 milliliters) gin

1 ounce (30 milliliters)
fresh lemon juice

1 ounce (30 milliliters)
simple syrup (recipe
on page 12)

soda water, to top glass

Garnish: slice lemon

◆ Fill a collins glass with a handful of ice. Add in the gin, lemon juice, and simple syrup and combine. Top with soda water and stir gently. Garnish with a slice of lemon.

Mimosa

For those who want to be at the top of their class, this is the cocktail for you. Simple to make and always a hit, this popular cocktail looks elegant and definitely won't make anyone S.P.E.W. (but remember, it's mimOsa, not mimosA)!

Serves: 1
Preparation time: 5 minutes
Glassware: Champagne flute

2 ½ ounces
(75 milliliters)
orange juice
2 ½ ounces
(75 milliliters)
sparkling wine
Garnish: orange wedge

◆ Combine the chilled orange juice and sparkling wine in a champagne flute. Garnish with an orange wedge.

Magic Duel

Magic Duel is a tasty twist on the classic Moscow Mule. Undefeatable in its perfect pairing of sweet and citrus flavors, it is said to be the greatest cocktail creation of all time. Prepare to be schooled in the art of mixology with this unbeatable beverage!

Serves: 1
Preparation time: 5 minutes
Glassware: Copper mug

4 ounces
(120 milliliters)
cloudy apple cider

1½ ounces
(45 milliliters)
vodka

2 ounces
(120 milliliters)
ginger beer

½ ounce
(15 milliliters) fresh
lemon juice

pinch ground ginger

ice cubes

Garnish: apple slices on
a cocktail stick and
lemon wheels

◆ In a cocktail shaker, combine the cider, vodka, ginger beer, and lemon juice with a pinch of ground ginger and a handful of ice cubes. Shake until cool and pour into the mug. Garnish with apple slices on a cocktail stick and lemon wheels.

Bellini-Trix

The Bellini-Trix is a strange and dark cocktail that is great for serving at any family reunion, especially if your family tree is in need of some seriously heavy pruning! Don't fret, after a few glasses of bubbly, everyone will be cackling in delight and putting family feuds to bed.

Serves: 6
Preparation time: 30 minutes
Glassware: Champagne flute

1 (14 ounces/ 390 grams) jar cherries in kirsch
16 ounces (500 milliliters) fresh cherry juice
4 tablespoons caster sugar
pinch edible glitter
slice lemon
1 bottle prosecco or Champagne
Garnish: 2 black cherries on a cocktail stick

◆ Place the liquid from the cherries in kirsch and the fresh cherry juice into a small saucepan. Bring to a boil, then simmer for about 20 minutes until reduced by approximately one third. Leave the black cherry mixture to cool. Once cool, add the cherries back to the saucepan and blend using a hand blender. Cover and refrigerate for 1 to 2 days until needed.

◆ To make the cocktail, mix sugar and edible glitter. Use a slice of lemon to rim the edge of a Champagne flute and dip the rim in the sugar/edible glitter mixture (learn how to rim a glass on page 5). Fill the glass one-third full with the black cherry puree and top with prosecco or Champagne. Garnish with a black cherry on a cocktail stick.

GHOSTLY GULPS

Bloodier than Mary

This rather ghoulish looking cocktail is more than it seems. Don't let its appearance scare your guests away, as this cocktail is simply delicious and won't last long. Grab a glass before it vanishes into thin air!

Serves: 2
Preparation time: 10 minutes
Glassware: Pitcher and mason jar

crushed ice

3½ ounces (100 milliliters) vodka

17½ ounces (500 milliliters) tomato juice

½ ounce (15 milliliters) fresh lemon juice

Few shakes Worcestershire sauce

Few shakes Tabasco

Pinch celery salt

Pinch black pepper

Garnish: 2 celery sticks, 1 slice lemon

◆ Place crushed ice in a pitcher and pour in the vodka, tomato juice, and lemon juice over the ice. Add in Worcestershire sauce, Tabasco, celery salt, and pepper. Stir until the outside of the pitcher feels cold. Serve in a mason jar and garnish with celery sticks and sliced lemon.

Nearly Legless Nick

This strong cocktail is a mix of many spirits and can certainly pack quite a punch. After a few of these, you don't need to be a natural at divination to know that you won't be able to dance in a straight line!

Serves: 1
Preparation time: 5 minutes
Glassware: Collins glass

1½ ounces
   (45 milliliters) light
   rum
½ ounce
   (15 milliliters) dark
   rum
½ ounce
   (15 milliliters)
   orgeat
¾ ounce
   (22.5 milliliters)
   orange curaçao
1 ounce (30 milliliters)
   fresh lime juice
ice cubes
1 teaspoon grenadine
Garnish: mint leaves and
   orange wedge

◆ In a cocktail shaker, combine the rums, orgeat, orange curaçao, and lime juice with a handful of ice cubes. Shake until the mixture is cool. Strain into a collins glass filled with more ice cubes. Slowly pour in the grenadine using the side of the glass to color the drink (learn how to layer ingredients on page 5). Garnish with mint leaves and an orange wedge.

Port-Ergeist

Those who don't get a taste of this cheeky little cocktail will be peeved. Both hearty and refreshing, the Port–Ergeist will definitely deliver a night of mischief and unruly fun!

Serves: *1*
Preparation time: *5 minutes*
Glassware: *Rocks glass*

1 ounce (30 milliliters) gin

1 ounce (30 milliliters) ruby port

¾ ounce (22 milliliters) fresh lemon juice

½ ounce (15 milliliters) cinnamon syrup (recipe on page 13)

1 teaspoon cranberry preserves

ice cubes

crushed ice

Garnish: mint sprig and skewered blackberry and raspberry

◆ In a cocktail shaker, combine the gin, port, lemon juice, cinnamon syrup, and cranberry preserves with a handful of ice cubes and shake until chilled. Strain over crushed ice in a rocks glass. Garnish with a mint sprig and skewered blackberry and raspberry.

The Raven

This elegant and sophisticated cocktail is perfect for the discerning drinker who prizes keeping their wits beyond measure. Let this drink work its subtle magic and, once consumed, even the most aloof of drinkers will come out of their shell and be the life of the party.

Serves: 1
Preparation time: 5 minutes
Glassware: Coupe glass

1½ ounces
(45 milliliters) gin

¾ ounce
(22.5 milliliters)
triple sec

¾ ounce
(22.5 milliliters)
fresh lemon juice

½ ounce
(15 milliliters) egg
whites

ice cubes

Garnish: lemon twist

◆ In a cocktail shaker, combine the gin, triple sec, fresh lemon juice, and egg whites along with a handful of ice cubes. Shake until cold and strain into a coupe glass. Garnish with a lemon twist.

Sweet Treats

Fizzing Sweet Treats

Inspired by one of Honeydukes's most popular sweets, this cocktail harnesses the sherbetty goodness of Queenbee's Fizzing Whizzbees to create a fantastic fizzing sensation. Save up all your pocket money and raid the local candy store, as this cocktail is all about the sweet treats!

Serves: *1*
Preparation time: *15 minutes*
Glassware: *Coupe glass*

1 packet sherbet
   powder, to rim glass

2 ounces
   (60 milliliters) gin

½ ounce
   (15 milliliters)
   honey syrup (recipe
   on page 12)

¾ ounce
   (22.5 milliliters)
   fresh lemon juice

ice cubes

Garnish: lollipop as a
   cocktail stirrer

◆ First, rim a glass with sherbet powder (learn how to rim a glass on page 5). In a cocktail shaker, combine the gin, honey syrup, and lemon juice along with a handful of ice cubes. Shake until cold and strain into a coupe glass. Garnish with a lollipop as a cocktail stirrer.

Chocolate Hopper

The mood-enhancing properties of chocolate are well known. For a guaranteed party winner, conjure up these chocolate frog–inspired drinks and leave guests hopping with joy.

Serves: 2
Preparation time: 45–60 minutes
Glassware: Martini glass

For the Chocolate Ganache

8 ounces (230 milliliters) heavy cream

5 ounces (140 grams) semi-sweet chocolate, chopped

For the Cocktail

4 tablespoons grated chocolate, to rim glass + to garnish

ice cubes

chocolate ganache

1 ounce (30 milliliters) vodka

4 ounces (120 milliliters) Irish cream

◆ To make the ganache, in a pot heat the heavy cream over medium high heat until it starts to boil. Then, pour the heavy cream over the chopped chocolate in a medium-sized bowl and stir until the chocolate melts. Allow to fully cool down before adding to the cocktail to avoid splitting the mixture.

◆ To make the cocktail, rim a martini glass with grated chocolate (learn how to rim a glass on page 5). Next, fill a cocktail shaker with ice cubes and add in the chocolate ganache, vodka, and Irish cream. Shake vigorously until cool and strain into the rimmed martini glass. Garnish with more grated chocolate.

Every Flavor Jelly Shots

These jelly shots are essential for any party. With endless options for flavors, you can have real fun creating these little tasty treats. Your partygoers will enjoy tasting them as much as you enjoy conjuring them!

Serves: 10+ (20 shots)
Preparation time:
8 hours, for setting
Glassware: Shot glasses
or novelty test tubes

2.2 ounces
   (60 grams) jelly
   beans
10 ounces
   (300 milliliters)
   vodka
1½ tablespoons
   gelatin powder
1 cup (200 grams)
   sugar
½ teaspoon citric
   acid powder

◆ Place 2 to 3 jelly beans of the same color into each shot glass or test tube and pour ⅓ ounce/10 milliliters vodka on top. Cover and set aside for 48 hours to allow the jelly beans to infuse into the vodka. Once the vodka has been infused, carefully remove the jelly beans from the shot glass.

◆ Next, pour the gelatin powder into a mixing bowl, add ½ to ¾ cup/150 milliliters cold water, and set aside for 10 to 15 minutes until all the water is absorbed.

◆ Heat 1½ cups/350 milliliters water with the sugar and citric acid powder in a saucepan, stirring occasionally to dissolve all ingredients. Remove from the heat when you notice vapors appearing above the water. Add in the soaked gelatin and stir until it is completely dissolved. Leave to cool at room temperature. When the mixture becomes clear and the foam disappears from the surface, it is ready to add to the shot glasses with the infused vodka. Cover and chill for up to 8 hours or overnight before serving.

◆ For a truly "every flavor" experience, you can also infuse one or two of your shots with less appetizing flavors such as chili or coffee!

Licorice Wand

There is an old bartender's prophecy that the drink chooses the drinker. If this drink chooses you, a great night is to be expected! While this cocktail may look like it contains some dark and powerful magic, you will find its true nature to be both sweet and revitalizing.

Serves: 1
Preparation time: 5 minutes
Glassware: Rocks glass

1½ ounces
   (45 milliliters)
   absinthe

ice cubes

Cola, to top glass

Garnish: licorice stick
   (wand!)

◆ Pour the absinthe into a rocks glass filled with a handful of ice cubes. Top with cola, garnish with a licorice stick, and give it a stir.

PARTY PLEASURES

Tempting Fruit Forest

Everyone knows that when something is forbidden, it is all the more tempting, which is definitely the case with this cocktail! The Tempting Fruit Forest not only tastes delicious, but also has many mystical secrets hiding between the mint leaves. Grab some friends, drink up, and try not to stray from the path . . .

Serves: 6-8
Preparation time: 10 minutes
Glassware: Pitcher and mason jars

2 lemons, thin sliced

2 limes, thin sliced

1 orange, thin sliced

several mint leaves + extra to garnish

6 ounces (180 milliliters) agave nectar

5 ounces (120 milliliters) light tequila

2 ounces (60 milliliters) fresh lime juice

1 (750 milliliters) bottle red wine

soda water, to top glass

◆ Add the fruit, mint, agave nectar, tequila, lime juice, and red wine to a large pitcher. Give the mixture a vigorous stir and top with soda water. Allow the cocktail to chill in the fridge for at least an hour before serving. To serve, pour the cocktail into mason jars and garnish with more mint leaves.

Brain Blaster

These cocktail shots are the perfect treat for any magical gathering that wants to kick things up a notch. The eerie appearance of this drink calls for bravery, as you need to be brave at heart to give it a try.

Serves: 1
Preparation time: 5 minutes
Glassware: Shot glass

1 ounce (30 milliliters) chilled peach schnapps

1 teaspoon Irish cream liqueur

1 teaspoon grenadine

◆ Pour the chilled schnapps into a shot glass. Very gently pour the Irish cream liqueur over the schnapps. Wait until the Irish cream liqueur begins to clump and "curdle," to look like a brain. Finally, gently pour the grenadine down the side of the shot glass.

Fluttering Flute

This cocktail glitters, shimmers, and flutters, making it a real catch! Wow your guests and go for the gold with this luxurious cocktail to score maximum party points.

Serves: *1*
Preparation time: *10 minutes*
Glassware: *Champagne flute*

½ ounce
  (15 milliliters)
  elderflower cordial
2 ounces
  (60 milliliters)
  pressed apple juice
chilled prosecco, to
  top glass
pinch edible glitter
  (preferably gold)
Garnish: skewered
  Ferrero Rocher®
  Chocolate and
  strawberry

◆ To make the cocktail, combine the elderflower cordial and apple juice in a Champagne flute. Top with chilled prosecco, add a pinch of edible glitter, and give the cocktail a gentle stir. Garnish with skewered Ferrero Rocher® Chocolate and strawberry.

◆ To make the garnish, draw some wings on white paper and cut them out. Place your set of wings underneath the Ferrero Rocher® Chocolate sticker and use a small piece of tape to secure the wings to the Ferrero Rocher® Chocolate. With a cocktail stick, skewer the Ferrero Rocher® Chocolate and the strawberry.

Merrymaking Elixir

Guffaw and gulp, shriek and sip with this miracle merrymaking elixir! It's the perfect remedy to liven up any party, sparking merriment and tomfoolery in all who drink it. For being such a small cocktail, Merrymaking Elixir's three colorful layers make it a real stunner.

Serves: *1*
Preparation time: *5 minutes*
Glassware: *Shot glass*

1 ounce (30 milliliters) raspberry vodka

1 ounce (30 milliliters) sour mix

ice cubes

½ ounce (15 milliliters) grenadine

½ ounce (15 milliliters) blue curaçao

◆ In a cocktail shaker, combine the vodka and sour mix with a handful of ice cubes. Shake vigorously until the mixture is cool and pour it into a shot glass. Pour the grenadine slowly down the inside of the glass and allow it to sink to the bottom (learn how to layer ingredients on page 5). Layer in the blue curaçao and allow it to sink to the middle of the glass (it should sit on top of the grenadine if poured slowly down the inside of the glass). The finished product should have three layers: red, blue, and white, from bottom to top.

Winning Shot

When you're celebrating an athletic victory, this adrenaline-fueled cocktail is designed to help you score and keep you going till dawn!

Serves: 1
Preparation time: 5 minutes
Glassware: Two shot glasses and a pint glass

1 ounce (30 milliliters) vodka

1 ounce (30 milliliters) Jägermeister

4 ounces (120 milliliters) energy drink

◆ Fill two shot glasses, one with vodka and the other with Jägermeister. Pour the energy drink into a pint glass. Take the Jägermeister shot first, then drop the vodka shot into the pint glass and drink up.

Mischievous Punch

This party perfect punch will definitely bring out the mischievous side in all who drink it. Both pink and glittery, it is a surefire way to enchant your guests, so grab a glass and let the magic commence.

Serves: 6–8
Preparation time: 5 minutes
Glassware: Large pitcher or cauldron

ice cubes

6 ounces (180 milliliters) vodka

3 ounces (90 milliliters) fresh lime juice

3 ounces (90 milliliters) cranberry juice

2 ounces (60 milliliters) coconut rum

1.25 liters pink lemonade

1 pinch edible glitter

Garnish: lemon wheels

◆ In a large pitcher or cauldron filled with ice, combine all the ingredients, and give it a good mix before serving. Garnish with lemon wheels and serve in your glassware of choice.

ADVANCED POTIONS

Advanced Potion

Containing what first appears to be floating eyes of newts, this cocktail produces a truly magical lava lamp phenomenon! Conjure up mystical bubbles that pop in your mouth to release hidden flavor.

Serves: 8+
Preparation time: 30-45 minutes
Glassware: Wine glass

For the Mystical Bubbles

3½ ounces
  (100 milliliters) Sourz
  Apple liqueur

1 gram food-grade sodium
  alginate made from
  seaweed extracts

1 (12-ounce) bottle water
  (if calcium content of
  tap water is too high, the
  reverse spherification
  won't work)

1 gram food-grade calcium
  lactate

1 pipette

For the Cocktail

1 ounce (30 milliliters)
  vodka

lemonade, to top glass

◆ To make the mystical bubbles, in a bowl combine the Sourz Apple liqueur with the sodium alginate and mix together with a whisk or fork. This process can take 10 to 15 minutes, as the sodium alginate can take some time to fully dissolve. Once dissolved, set aside until most of the bubbles are gone; this should result in a thick mixture.

◆ Next, fill a shallow baking tray with bottled water and dissolve the calcium lactate by gently stirring. Fill a pipette with the Sourz Apple mixture and carefully allow single drops to fall into the water from a height of approximately 6 inches/15 centimeters above the water's surface. The mixture should immediately solidify when it hits the water's surface, forming solid spheres with liquid centers.

◆ Continue this process until the desired number of spheres has been achieved, then carefully fish them out with a fork or small sieve and place them in a jar or resealable Tupperware. Once all the spheres are formed, gently place them in a sieve and wash with water, then add them to a jar or Tupperware submerged with Sourz Apple until required. The cocktail bubbles can be stored in the refrigerator for up to 1 month.

◆ To make the cocktail, place several spheres in a wine glass, add vodka, and top with lemonade. The spheres should float up and down the glass to create a lava lamp effect before settling at the surface.

Lethal Elixir

This clear, smooth liquid may look innocuous, but its mix of spirits make it extremely lethal. Excel in potions class with this delicious concoction.

Serves: *1*
Preparation time: *5 minutes*
Glassware: *Coupe or novelty glass beaker*

¾ ounces (22 milliliters) absinthe

¾ ounces (22 milliliters) elderflower liqueur

¾ ounces (22 milliliters) Lillet Blanc

¾ ounces (22 milliliters) fresh lemon juice

dash (1 milliliter) gin

ice cubes

dry ice pellets (to give it that fresh-from-the-cauldron vibe)

◆ In a cocktail shaker, combine the absinthe, elderflower liqueur, Lillet Blanc, lemon juice, and gin with a handful of ice cubes. Shake until contents are cool and strain into a coupe glass or novelty glass beaker. Carefully add a couple of dry ice pellets* before serving.

---

*When using dry ice pellets, please follow guidance stated in Elf and Safety on page 17.

Green-Eyed Potion

This vivid green drink looks positively spooky but tastes great and gives you an extra boost of confidence. It will bring its drinker right out of their shell, as if they are embodying a totally different person . . .

Serves: 1
Preparation time: 5 minutes
Glassware: Martini glass

¾ ounce
(23.5 milliliters)
Crème de Cacao

¾ ounce
(23.5 milliliters)
Crème de Menthe

¾ ounce
(23.5 milliliters)
light cream

ice cubes

Garnish: mint leaf

◆ In a cocktail shaker, combine the Crème de Cacao, Crème de Menthe, and light cream with a handful of ice cubes and shake until cool. Strain the cocktail into a martini glass and garnish with a mint leaf.

Most Potently Potent Love Potion

Cast to your heart's desire with this gorgeously enchanting cocktail. Rumored to be the strongest love potion of its kind, this Most Potently Potent Love Potion is a foolproof way to get the romance flowing between you and a special someone, so drink up and watch the sparks fly!

Serves: 4
Preparation time: 5 *minutes*
Glassware: Wine glass

1 (750 milliliters)
   bottle rosé wine
2 ounces
   (60 milliliters)
   strawberry syrup
   (recipe on page 14)
2 ounces
   (60 milliliters) fresh
   lemon juice
2 ounces
   (60 milliliters) gin
Garnish: fresh
   strawberry, halved

◆ Pour the rosé into an ice cube tray and freeze overnight. In a blender, combine the rosé cubes, strawberry syrup, lemon juice, and gin and blend for 2 minutes or until smooth. Pour into a wine glass and garnish with a halved strawberry.

Loose-Lipped Libation

This crystal-clear cocktail can make the drinker very loose-lipped. With an eye of newt (olive), this cocktail classic should be in everybody's standard book of spell-tacular cocktails.

Serves: 1
Preparation time: 5 minutes
Glassware: Martini glass

2 ounces
    (60 milliliters)
    vodka
½ ounce
    (15 milliliters) dry
    vermouth
ice cubes
Garnish: eye of newt
    (olive)

◆ In a cocktail shaker, combine the vodka and dry vermouth with a handful of ice cubes. Shake until cool, then strain into a martini glass and garnish with an olive.

Babbling Beverage

This cocktail bewitches the mind and ensnares the senses, causing the drinker to babble nonsense throughout the night (well, after a few of these, at any rate!). This is the perfect potion to serve whenever you want to get the conversation flowing.

Serves: 1
Preparation time: 5 minutes
Glassware: Martini glass

1½ ounces
   (45 milliliters)
   vodka

³⁄₅ ounce
   (20 milliliters)
   raspberry liqueur

2 ounces
   (60 milliliters)
   pineapple juice

ice cubes

◆ In a cocktail shaker, combine the vodka, raspberry liqueur, and pineapple juice with a handful of ice cubes. Shake until cool, then strain into a martini glass.

Delicious Draught

Relieve your aching bones with this sweet and sophisticated drink. This special draught is guaranteed to bring glamour and elegance to any cocktail party—without costing you an arm and a leg!

Serves: *1*
Preparation time: *5 minutes*
Glassware: *Martini glass*

2 ounces (60 milliliters) bourbon whiskey

1 ounce (30 milliliters) rosso vermouth

2 dashes (2 milliliters) angostura bitters

ice cubes

Garnish: maraschino cherry and lemon twist

◆ In a cocktail shaker, combine the bourbon, vermouth, and bitters with a handful of ice cubes. Shake until cool, then strain into a martini glass. Garnish with a cherry and lemon twist.

Lucky Liquid

This fizzy golden delight will give you an extra boost of confidence to handle whatever the night throws at you. Drink up, it's going to be your lucky night!

Serves: 1
Preparation time: 5 minutes
Glassware: Champagne flute

¹/₃ ounce
   (10 milliliters)
   simple syrup (recipe
   on page 12)

¹/₃ ounce
   (10 milliliters)
   lemon juice

1¹/₂ ounces
   (45 milliliters)
   ginger beer

pinch edible glitter
   (preferably gold)

Champagne or other
   sparkling wine, to
   top glass

Garnish: flakes edible
   gold leaf (for an
   extra special touch)

◆ In a Champagne flute, gently mix the simple syrup, lemon juice, and ginger beer. Add in a pinch of edible glitter and top with Champagne or sparkling wine. If you're feeling extra lucky, garnish the surface with flakes of edible gold leaf.

Dark and Divine Drinks

Soul-Sucking Kiss

Based on the classic Vampire's Kiss, this cocktail is equally as powerful and if anything, a bit darker! Pucker up and sink your teeth into this fruity and rejuvenating cocktail, but be careful not to trade your soul away for another . . .

Serves: 1
Preparation time: 5 minutes
Glassware: Martini glass

2 tablespoons sugar
1 drop red food coloring
1½ ounces
   (45 milliliters) vodka
½ ounce (15 milliliters)
   raspberry liqueur +
   extra to garnish
1½ ounces
   (45 milliliters)
   chilled Champagne or
   sparkling white wine
Garnish: red sugar, to rim
   glass

◆ In a mortar and pestle, grind the sugar with the red food coloring. Rim a martini glass (learn how to rim a glass on page 5) with the red sugar. Pour the vodka and raspberry liqueur into a martini glass and top up with the chilled Champagne or sparkling wine. To garnish, pour in a small amount of raspberry liqueur over the back of a spoon so that it floats on top of the drink.

Dark Magic

Like the dark arts themselves, this cocktail comes with lots of warnings. Therefore, handle with care and don't let the darkness consume you! Watch how the smallest amount of Peruvian Instant Darkness Powder (activated charcoal powder) transforms this drink, plunging it into darkness.

Serves: 1
Preparation time: 5 minutes
Glassware: Coupe glass

1½ ounces (45 milliliters) light rum

¼ teaspoon activated charcoal powder*

½ ounce (15 milliliters) fresh lemon juice

½ ounce (15 milliliters) fresh lime juice

1 ounce (30 milliliters) simple syrup (recipe on page 12)

¼ ounce (7.5 milliliters) maraschino liqueur

ice cubes

dry ice pellets

◆ In a cocktail shaker, combine the rum, activated charcoal powder, lemon and lime juices, simple syrup, and maraschino liqueur along with a handful of ice cubes. Shake until cold and strain into a coupe glass. Add some dry ice pellets** to give it an extra spooky effect before serving.

---

*See guidance on activated charcoal powder in Elf and Safety on page 17.

**When using dry ice pellets, please follow guidance stated in Elf and Safety on page 17.

You-Know-Woo-Woo

The cocktail that cannot be named (well, after you've drunk a few of them, anyway!). This fun cocktail is super easy to brew—and tastes scrumptious, too! Perfect for a night of drinking with your witches.

Serves: 1
Preparation time: 5 minutes
Glassware: Martini glass

1 ounce (30 milliliters) vodka

1 ounce (30 milliliters) peach schnapps

2 ounces (60 milliliters) cranberry juice

ice cubes

Garnish: lime wheel

◆ In a cocktail shaker, combine the vodka, schnapps, and cranberry juice along with a handful of ice cubes. Shake until cool, then strain into a martini glass. Garnish with a lime wheel.

Grim-Old Fashioned

This cocktail is for the serious witch or wizard who needs to mull over life's big issues while staring moodily into a smoldering fire. Whether it is worrying over exam results, problems of the heart, or the impending sense of doom that lurks around every corner, look no further because this is the drink for you!

Serves: 1
Preparation time: 5 minutes
Glassware: Rocks glass

¼ ounce
   (7.5 milliliters)
   simple syrup (recipe
   on page 12)

½ teaspoon
   (2 milliliters)
   angostura bitters

1 teaspoon
   (4 milliliters) water

ice cube

2 ounces
   (60 milliliters)
   bourbon whiskey

Garnish: orange peel

♦ In a rocks glass, combine the simple syrup, bitters, and water. Add an ice cube and stir in the bourbon. Garnish with an orange peel.

Death Beeters

Conjure up the Death Beeters cocktail and anyone you serve it to will remain loyal. This unique drink derives its vivid color from natural beetroot dyes. Fresh ginger makes this lightly spiced cocktail a champion of flavors as well as a healthy addition to your five-a-day.

Serves: 4
Preparation time: 10 minutes
Glassware: Martini glass

3 baby beetroots,
   peeled and steamed
1 medium apple, cored
1 inch
   (2.5 centimeters)
   fresh ginger, peeled
   and thinly sliced
5 ounces
   (140 milliliters)
   water
6 ounces
   (180 milliliters)
   vodka
2 ounces
   (60 milliliters)
   ginger syrup (recipe
   on page 13)
2 ounces
   (60 milliliters) fresh
   lime juice
ice cubes
Garnish: lemon slice

◆ In a blender, combine the beetroots, apple, and ginger with the water and blend until smooth. Pass the mixture through a fine mesh sieve and add more water until the mixture reaches a juice-like consistency.

◆ In a cocktail shaker, combine the blended juice with vodka, ginger syrup, and lime juice with ice cubes. Shake the cocktail until cold. Strain the cocktail into a martini glass and garnish with a lemon slice.

Deadly Negroni

Hypnotic and smooth as any serpent, this brooding classic is perfect for sipping in dark corners while concocting your master plan to take over the wizarding world! Like any dark scheme, this cocktail is best served ice cold.

Serves: *1*
Preparation time: *5 minutes*
Glassware: *Rocks glass*

ice cubes

1 ounce (30 milliliters) dry gin

1 ounce (30 milliliters) Campari

1 ounce (30 milliliters) sweet vermouth

large novelty ice cube (the bigger the better)

Garnish: citrus twist

◆ Half fill a cocktail shaker with ice cubes, add in the gin, Campari, and sweet vermouth, and stir until the shaker is cold to the touch. Add a large novelty ice cube to a rocks glass and strain in the ingredients from the cocktail shaker. Garnish with a citrus twist.

Cold Rum Cauldron

This simple cocktail tastes divine while looking dark 'n stormy. Ideal for a hot summer's day, this drink is a great way to stay cool while embracing your inner dark side.

Serves: *1*
Preparation time: *5 minutes*
Glassware: *Collins glass*

2 scoops vanilla ice cream

2 ounces (60 milliliters) dark rum

Ginger beer, to top glass

Garnish: lime wheel

◆ Add the vanilla ice cream to a collins glass and pour in the dark rum. Top with ginger beer and garnish with a lime wheel.

Snakebite

This muggle coming-of-age cocktail classic is served at many a student party. Favored by those who are cunning and resourceful, it is cheap and simple to make.

Serves: 1
Preparation time: 5 minutes
Glassware: Pint glass

½ ounce
(15 milliliters)
blackcurrant cordial

10 ounces (½ pint)
stout beer

10 ounces (½ pint)
cider

◆ To a pint glass, first add a layer of blackcurrant cordial. Next, add the stout beer. Then, finish with the cider to form distinct layers (learn how to layer ingredients on page 5).

BOTANICAL BEVERAGES

Floral D'Liqueur

This cocktail is pink, gorgeous, and essential for any girls' night out! The Floral D'Liqueur not only looks breathtakingly beautiful, but is also a real champion, too.

Serves: 1
Preparation time: 5 minutes
Glassware: Martini glass

1½ ounces (45 milliliters) lemon vodka

½ ounce (15 milliliters) triple sec

½ ounce (15 milliliters) fresh lime juice

1 ounce (30 milliliters) cranberry juice

ice cubes

Garnish: edible flowers and edible glitter

◆ In a cocktail shaker, combine the vodka, triple sec, fresh lime juice, and cranberry juice along with a handful of ice cubes. Shake until cold and strain into a martini glass. Garnish with edible flowers and edible glitter.

Long-Lost Love

This cocktail is for all the hopeless romantics out there who, after all this time, have not given up on finding that special someone. As a very wise wizard once said, having the ability to love is the most powerful magic there is.

Serves: 1
Preparation time: 15 minutes
Glassware: Collins glass

½ ounce
    (15 milliliters)
    raspberry cordial
2 ounces
    (60 milliliters) gin
¼ teaspoon rose water
1 ounce (30 milliliters)
    fresh lemon juice
ice cubes
pink lemonade, to top
    glass
Garnish: rose petals and
    mint sprig

For the Cocktail

◆ In a cocktail shaker. combine the raspberry cordial (recipe below), gin, rose water, and lemon juice. Next, add in a handful of ice cubes and shake until cool. Strain the cocktail into a collins glass and top with pink lemonade. Garnish with rose petals and a mint sprig.

For the Raspberry Cordial

4 ounces (120 grams) fresh raspberries
2½ ounces (75 milliliters) water
2½ ounces (75 grams) demerara sugar
zest of 1 whole lemon

◆ In a saucepan, combine the ingredients and simmer on medium heat until the raspberries start to break up. Remove from the heat and allow to cool. Once cool, strain through a fine sieve. The raspberry cordial can be stored in a sterilized bottle and kept refrigerated for up to 1 month.

The Whomping Limoncello

This cocktail is a real heavy hitter with the perfect blend of sweet and sour flavors. With floral garnishes of mint and cucumber, this citrus–inspired drink is ideal for enjoying on a hot summer's day while sunbathing on the grass. Get ready to be impressed by this knockout of a cocktail.

Serves: *1*
Preparation time: *5 minutes*
Glassware: *Collins glass*

1 ounce (30 milliliters)
  limoncello
1 ounce (30 milliliters)
  gin
ice cubes
crushed ice
lemonade, to top glass
Garnish: lemon wheel,
  sliced cucumber,
  and fresh thyme
  sprig

◆ Combine the limoncello and gin in a cocktail shaker with a handful of ice cubes. Shake until cool and strain into a collins glass with some crushed ice. Top with lemonade and garnish with a lemon wheel, sliced cucumber, and thyme sprig.

The Botanist's Iced Tea

This cocktail has been given a botanical twist on the classic.
Enjoy this bewitching combination of four different white spirits and triple sec.

Serves: *1*
Preparation time: *10 minutes*
Glassware: *Collins glass*

½ ounce (15 milliliters)
   light rum
½ ounce (15 milliliters)
   gin
½ ounce (15 milliliters)
   vodka
½ ounce (15 milliliters)
   light tequila
½ ounce (15 milliliters)
   triple sec
½ ounce (15 milliliters)
   simple syrup (recipe on
   page 12)
½ ounce (15 milliliters)
   fresh lemon juice
½ ounce (15 milliliters)
   fresh lime juice
ice cubes
Cola, to top glass
Garnish: mint sprig and
   lemon wheel

◆ In a cocktail shaker, combine the rum, gin, vodka, tequila, triple sec, simple syrup, lemon juice, and lime juice with a handful of ice cubes. Shake until cool and strain into a collins glass. Garnish with a mint sprig and lemon wheel.

Herbal Highball

An herbal remedy to warm the cockles of the heart, this twist on the classic cocktail packs a punch. Cast a spell with wafts of rosemary, luscious lavender, and zinging lemon.

Serves: 1
Preparation time: 10 minutes
Glassware: Collins glass

ice cubes

2 ounces
(60 milliliters)
bourbon whiskey

sparkling water, to top
glass

½ ounce
(15 milliliters) fresh
lemon juice

mint leaves

Garnish: lemon twist,
2 sprigs rosemary,
and 1 sprig lavender

◆ Fill a collins glass with ice, add the whiskey, and top with sparkling water. Add the lemon juice and mint leaves (rub between your palms first to release the essential oils).

◆ Garnish with a lemon twist and lavender sprig and stir to combine flavors. Finally, light the end of a rosemary sprig and immediately blow it out, then waft over the top of the glass and extinguish completely in a cup of water. Add in a fresh second rosemary sprig to complete the garnish.

Seasonal Sorcery

Witches' Brew

This cocktail is a real favorite for when there is a large gathering and you really can't help but show off your mixology skills! Dust off your cauldron and prepare to charm your partygoers with this spectacularly spooky delight.

Serves: 12–20
Preparation time: 10 minutes
Glassware: large punch bowl or novelty cauldron (to make a statement)

1 liter pineapple juice

1 liter orange juice

4–8 drops green or black food coloring

ice cubes

½ liter (500 milliliters) vodka

½ liter (500 milliliters) peach schnapps

1 (12-ounce) bottle lemonade

dry ice pellets* (for that freshly brewed potion effect)

◆ In a large punch bowl or cauldron, combine the pineapple juice, orange juice, food coloring, and ice. Next, add in the vodka, peach schnapps, and lemonade and stir gently. Carefully add in a few dry ice pellets to give your cocktail that freshly brewed potion effect.

---

* When using dry ice pellets, please follow guidance stated in Elf and Safety on page 17.

Pumpkin-Tini

This Pumpkin-Tini is the perfect accompaniment to any Halloween feast. The trick being that this cocktail does not contain any actual pumpkin, and the treat, of course, is its delicious taste!

Serves: 2
Preparation time: 5 minutes
Glassware: Martini glass

2 ripe passion fruits

2 ounces
(60 milliliters)
vanilla vodka

1 ounce (30 milliliters)
Passoã (passion fruit
liqueur)

1 tablespoon fresh lime
juice

1 tablespoon simple
syrup (recipe on
page 12)

ice cubes

prosecco, to top glass

Garnish: dried passion
fruit wheels

◆ Scoop the seeds from the passion fruits into a cocktail shaker. Then, add in the vodka, Passoã, lime juice, and simple syrup. Combine with a handful of ice cubes and shake vigorously until the mixture is cool. Strain into two martini glasses and top with prosecco. Garnish with dried passion fruit wheels.

Yule Punch

This icy blue winter drink captures the magic of the festive season perfectly. Put on your fanciest robes, pick a partner, and waltz into the night with this fantastic frozen cocktail!

Serves: *1*
Preparation time: *5 minutes*
Glassware: *Glass Goblet*

1 tablespoon maple/corn syrup, to rim glass

2 tablespoons desiccated coconut, to rim glass

crushed ice

2 ounces (60 milliliters) pineapple juice

1 ounce (30 milliliters) blue curaçao

1 ounce (30 milliliters) vodka

1 ounce (30 milliliters) cream of coconut

◆ Rim a glass goblet with maple/corn syrup and desiccated coconut (learn how to rim a glass on page 5). In a blender, combine two handfuls of crushed ice with the pineapple juice, blue curaçao, vodka, and cream of coconut. Blend the mixture until smooth and serve in the prepared glass.

Mulled Mead

This cocktail is perfect for getting everyone into the festive spirit while decorating for the holidays.
Whether you're hanging fairy lights or mistletoe, this is the winter warming cocktail for you.

Serves: 8
Preparation time: 20 minutes
Glassware: Glass goblet

25 ounces
(750 milliliters)
mead/cider

3 tablespoons brandy

8½ ounces
(250 milliliters)
apple juice

1 strip lemon peel

zest of 1 lemon

zest of 1 orange

sliced orange

½ teaspoon nutmeg

3 cloves

1 cinnamon stick

1 thumb-size piece
fresh ginger, sliced

Garnish: cinnamon stick

◆ Add all ingredients to a saucepan and gently warm through until simmering. Before serving, remove the whole spices, lemon peel, and orange slices using tongs or strain through a sieve. Garnish with a cinnamon stick.

Indulgent Eggnog

This rich cocktail is a true winter favorite. It's the perfect drink for sipping in front of a roaring fire after a long day of walking through the Scottish Highlands searching for magical creatures.

Serves: 4
Preparation time: 45 minutes
Glassware: Mason jars

2 eggs

6 teaspoons (25 grams) sugar

1 cup (240 milliliters) whole milk

½ cup (120 milliliters) heavy cream

3 ounces (90 milliliters) bourbon whiskey

2 ounces (60 milliliters) amaretto

1 tablespoon cinnamon + extra to top glass

Garnish: cinnamon sticks

◆ First, separate the eggs, keeping the egg whites and yolks in two separate large mixing bowls. Beat the egg yolks until they turn pale and yellow. Combine with the sugar and beat until the sugar is fully dissolved. Next, add the milk, cream, whiskey, amaretto, and cinnamon and stir gently.

◆ In the second bowl, beat the egg whites until they form stiff peaks. Gradually stir in the egg yolk mixture and allow the cocktail to chill in the fridge. Serve in mason jars and garnish with cinnamon sticks. Top with more ground cinnamon.

DRINKING GAME: THE GREAT BALL OF FIRE

No Potter-themed party is complete without a raucous drinking game, so invite your mates over and conjure up some fantastic cocktails to play the Great Ball of Fire: drinking edition!

HOW TO PLAY

You will need a standard pack of cards. This is a team game so all students must be divided into the four Hogwarts houses.

Place a tall glass in the middle of a table. This will be the central goblet. Surround the glass with a circle of cards facing down. Take it in turn to draw a card from the deck, with each card having a specific task assigned to it:

Ace: Duel
Choose someone to duel with and play a simple game of rock, paper, scissors. The loser must drink.

2: Expelliarmus
Last to yell this incantation and put their wand hand in the air must drink.

3: Veritaserum
This card triggers a "never have I ever" confession from the caster. All those who ever have must drink.

4: The Dark Lord
The caster who picks this card can only now be referred to as "You-Know-Who." Anyone who forgets this must drink.

(Continued on next page)

5: Aguamenti

Everyone at the table must start to drink and cannot stop drinking until the person to their left has stopped.

6: Sorting hat

The caster may choose a house of casters to drink.

7: Unbreakable vow

Choose a partner who must drink whenever you do.

8: House elf

Everyone in the house of the caster must swap one item of clothing. Those who refuse must drink.

9: Stupefy

Choose a person to drink and lose their turn.

10: 10 Points for _____!

Everyone drinks.

Jack: Confundus

Caster chooses a word, the next person says it and adds another, and so on. The first to get it wrong must drink.

Queen: Protego

Caster is immune from all group rules until the next Queen is drawn.

King: Contribute to the center goblet

The player to draw the final king must drink it all.

CONVERSION CHART

Term	Measurement (Imperial)	Measurement (Metric)
1 part	Any equal part	Any equal part
1 dash	$\frac{1}{32}$ ounce	1 milliliter
1 teaspoon	$\frac{1}{5}$ ounce	6 milliliters
1 tablespoon	$\frac{1}{6}$ ounce	5 milliliters
1 pony	$\frac{1}{2}$ ounce	15 milliliters
1 jigger/shot	1 ounce	30 milliliters
1 snit	3 ounces	90 milliliters
1 wine glass	4 ounces	120 milliliters
1 split	6 ounces	180 milliliters
1 cup	8 ounces	240 milliliters
1 pint	16 ounces	475 milliliters

Index